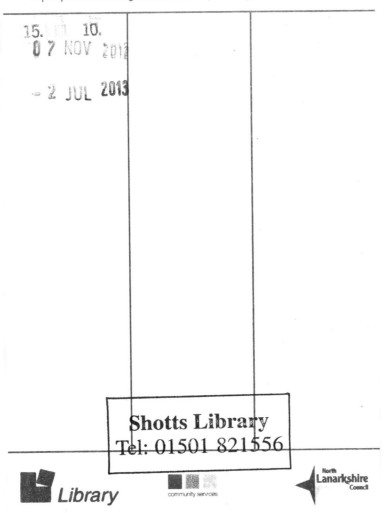

THE HUMAN BODY IN FOCUS

HOW WE GROW AND REPRODUCE

LIZ GOGERLY

Adapted from an original text by Michaela Miller

First published in 2009 by Franklin Watts

Franklin Watts
338 Euston Road
London NW1 3BH

Franklin Watts Australia
Level 17/207 Kent Street, Sydney, NSW 2000

Produced by Arcturus Publishing Limited,
26/27 Bickels Yard, 151–153 Bermondsey Street, London SE1 3HA

Understanding the Human Body is based on the series *Exploring the Human Body*, published by Franklin Watts.

Editor: Alex Woolf
Designer: Peta Phipps and Mike Reynolds
Illustrator: Michael Courtney
Picture researcher: Glass Onion Pictures
Consultant: Dr Kristina Routh

Picture Credits
Corbis: 29 (Gideon Mendel).
La Leche League International: 20.
Science Photo Library: 5 (Lea Paterson), 7 (BSIP, Laurent), 11 (Dr Yorgos Nikas), 13 (Ian Boddy), 15 (Dr G. Moscoso), 17 (Deep Light Productions), 18 (Ruth Jenkinson/MIDIRS), 21 (Ian Hooton), 23 (BSIP, Laurent), 25 (Damien Lovegrove), 26 (Gary Parker), 27 (BSIP, Laurent), 28 (Eye of Science).
Topfoto: 24 (John Powell).
Shutterstock: cover (Monkey Business Images).

A CIP catalogue record for this book is available from the British Library.

Dewey Decimal Classification Number: 612.6

ISBN 978 0 7496 9053 3

Printed in China

Franklin Watts is a division of Hachette Children's Books, an Hachette UK Company
www.hachette.co.uk

Contents

Creating Life

Reproduction is the creation of new life. Plants, animals and **bacteria** have different ways of reproducing. **Amoebae** are tiny creatures made of one cell. The cell splits in half to create more amoebae. This is called asexual reproduction. Other living things need a male and female to reproduce. The two sexes must join together to create new life. This is called sexual reproduction.

Hatching or birth?

The young of all creatures are born in different ways. Human beings are mammals. Like other mammals, the female gives birth to its young. Fish, amphibians, reptiles and insects lay eggs. Their young stay in the eggs until they are ready to hatch.

Love and babies

Human reproduction is complicated because we are social creatures. Feelings of attraction, love, care and respect are important to us. Partners usually have strong feelings for each other before they have babies.

Sexual awakening

The time when a human's body changes from a child's to an adult's is called puberty. Around this time many

This diagram shows asexual reproduction in an amoeba. Amoebae can only be seen under a microscope.

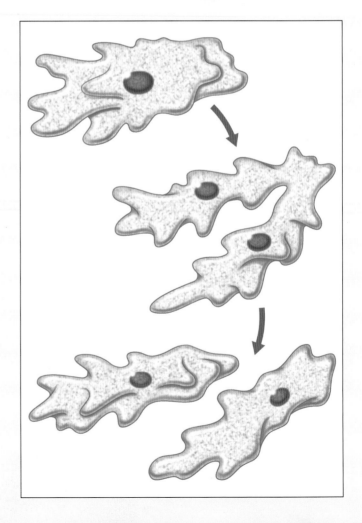

**Human babies
are produced
through sexual
reproduction.**

○

Q&A

How long does it take to reproduce?

The time it takes to reproduce is different for all creatures. Human females are usually pregnant for about 40 weeks. Elephants carry their babies for two years. Bird eggs take between two and eleven weeks to hatch. Eggs from small birds take less time to hatch than eggs from large birds.

young people think more about sex. This is totally natural. They are preparing themselves for sexual reproduction.

Being ready

It's important to think carefully before starting a sexual relationship. If a person is not ready for sex they may feel bad about themselves afterwards. Many diseases can be passed between sexual partners too. There is also the risk of getting pregnant and having an unplanned baby.

The **Female Reproductive System**

Females and males need reproductive **organs** to reproduce. A woman's reproductive organs are inside her body. Women have two ovaries, two **fallopian tubes** and a uterus (also called a womb). They also have an opening between the legs called the vagina. All of these organs are needed to create life.

Ovaries and eggs

The ovaries are rounded organs and measure about three centimetres long. They store hundreds of thousands of tiny eggs. Each egg is about the size of a pencil dot. These eggs are the female sex cells.

The egg's journey

The eggs travel along the fallopian tubes. Sometimes an egg joins with a male sex cell called a sperm. This is called fertilization.

The ovaries begin to release eggs when a girl reaches puberty. This happens because **hormones** in her blood tell the ovaries to release one egg. After that, an egg is released each month.

This diagram shows the female reproductive system.

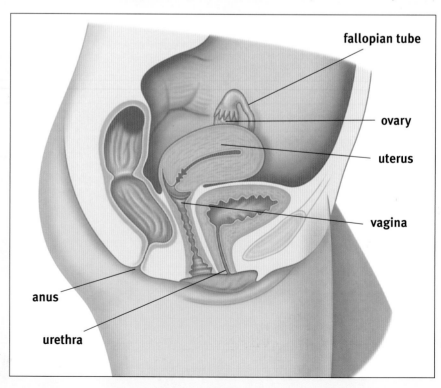

fallopian tube

ovary

uterus

vagina

anus

urethra

Preparing the uterus

Each month the uterus gets ready for a fertilized egg. It does this by making a soft lining rich in **blood vessels**. If the egg is not fertilized, the lining breaks down into blood. This blood leaves the body through the vagina.

Periods can be uncomfortable. Exercise, heat and medicine can help with the pain.

Menstruation

This bleeding is called menstruation, or a period. It happens about every 28 days. Most women stop having periods when they reach about 50. This means they are no longer fertile and cannot have babies.

○

Q&A

When do periods start?

Most girls begin their periods, between the ages of 11 and 13, although periods can begin earlier or later than this. Periods last about three to eight days.

The **Male Reproductive System**

The male reproductive **organs** are called the penis and testicles (or testes). These are outside a man's body. They hang between his legs. The two testicles are inside a bag of skin called the scrotum.

Sperm

Each testicle produces sperm. Sperm are the male sex cells. Boys begin to produce sperm around the age of ten to 12 years old. The testicles produce millions of sperm each day. The scrotum protects the testicles and the sperm.

Sperm are tiny cells. You need a microscope to see them. Sperm have a tadpole shape. They have round heads and long tails. Each sperm is about 0.05 millimetres long.

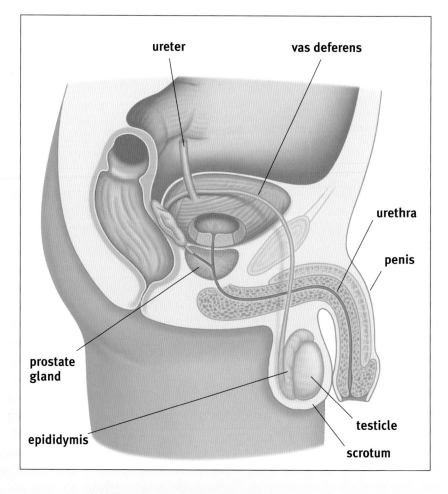

This diagram shows the male reproductive system.

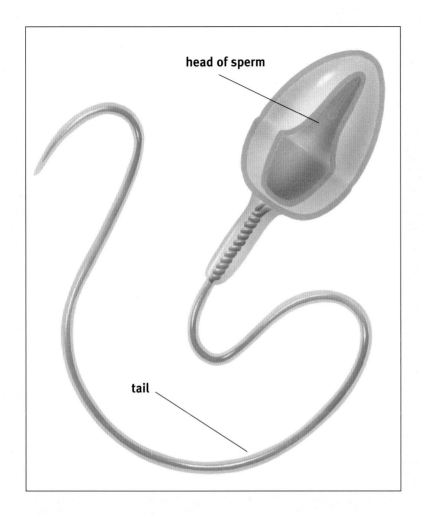

head of sperm

tail

This is a highly enlarged illustration of a sperm. They use their tails to move along.

The sperm's journey

Sperm travel to the penis from the testicles. Each testicle has its own tubes. Sperm are stored in a set of tubes called the epididymis. Sperm travel to the next set of tubes, called the vas deferens. Here the sperm mix with fluid. This mixture of fluid and sperm is called semen.

Semen

Semen travels through a tube in the penis called the urethra. Semen usually comes out of the penis when a man is sexually excited. This is called ejaculation. At this time the penis is hard. This is called an erection.

Q&A

What is a wet dream?

Many teenage boys have wet dreams. Often this is because they are sexually excited. A dream has 'turned them on'. This causes an erection and they ejaculate semen. The semen makes their sheets and clothes wet and sticky.

Making a Baby

To create a baby, sperm from a man needs to fertilize an egg from a woman. This usually happens when a man's penis and woman's vagina are joined together. This joining is called sexual intercourse.

Making love

When a couple have sex, their sexual organs begin to work. A man's penis becomes hard and erect. The woman's vagina becomes wet and slippery. This means the penis can slide easily inside her. The couple then move together so the penis slides in and out of the vagina.

Sperm begin to move through the male reproductive **organs** towards the penis. Eventually the man's penis ejaculates semen into the woman's vagina. A man ejaculates between two and five million sperm. The sperm swim up the vagina, into the uterus and towards the **fallopian tubes**.

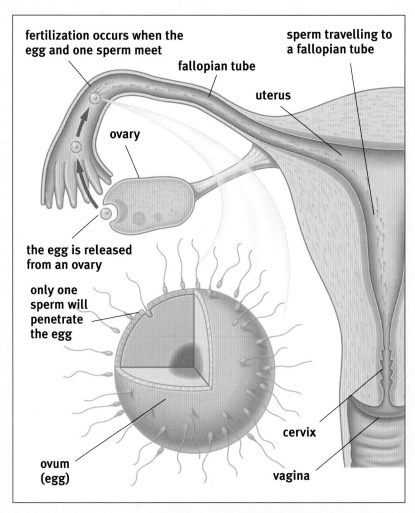

fertilization occurs when the egg and one sperm meet

sperm travelling to a fallopian tube

fallopian tube

uterus

ovary

the egg is released from an ovary

only one sperm will penetrate the egg

cervix

ovum (egg)

vagina

This diagram shows how sperm travel through the female reproductive organs to fertilize an egg.

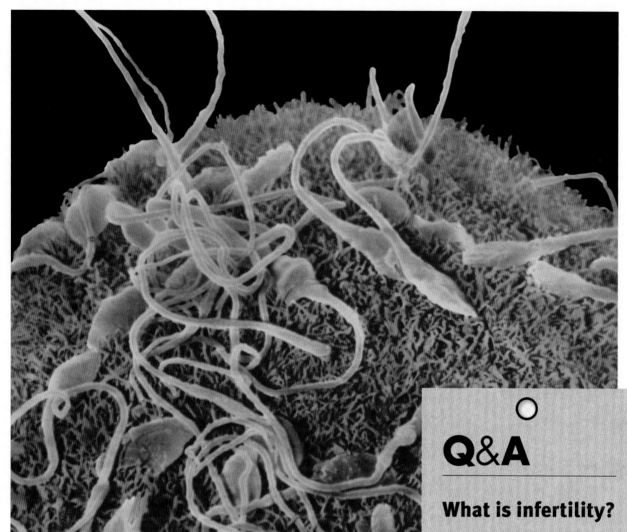

Hundreds of sperm surround the egg. Only one can join with the egg and start a new life.

The sperm race

Only one sperm will be successful and fertilize the egg. Each sperm races to join with the egg. The winning sperm burrows into the egg. A new life begins.

Perfect timing

Babies are not made every time a man and woman make love. Reproduction only happens if a sperm joins with an egg at the right time. This is within 24 to 36 hours of the eggs leaving the ovary for the fallopian tube.

Q&A

What is infertility?

Some people are never able to have their own children. A couple may have sexual intercourse but never reproduce. They are described as infertile. Usually, this is to do with the reproductive organs not working properly. Doctors can sometimes help these people to have babies.

Genes and Chromosomes

Eggs and sperm carry important information that is used to create the new baby. The information is contained in tiny packages called **genes**. Genes are passed on through families. A baby has the genes of his or her parents and grandparents, as well as the genes of family members who lived a long time ago.

Chromosomes

Genes are carried on **chromosomes**. Chromosomes are coiled strands of a chemical called **DNA** (deoxyribonucleic acid). Each egg and each sperm has 23 chromosomes. When an egg is fertilized, one cell is created. This cell contains 46 chromosomes and more than 100,000 genes. The cell multiplies into other cells. Each new cell contains the same 46 chromosomes and genes.

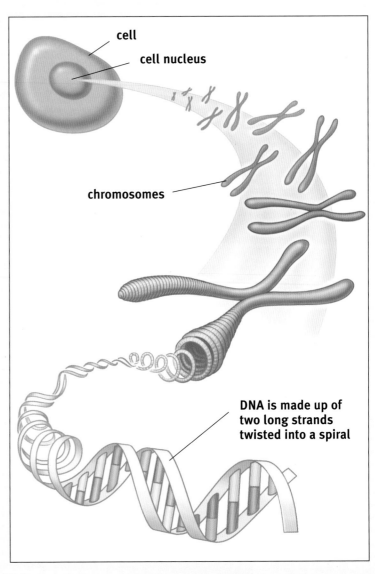

cell

cell nucleus

chromosomes

DNA is made up of two long strands twisted into a spiral

This diagram shows a cell and its chromosomes, which are made up of DNA. Genes lie along the chromosomes.

Boy or girl?

Genes decide the sex of a baby. Eggs and sperm contain a sex chromosome. Scientists call this X or Y. When an egg and sperm join together the sex chromosomes combine. Eggs can only have the X chromosome. Sperm can have either an X or a Y. If a sperm with an X chromosome joins with the egg, then a baby girl is made. If a sperm with a Y chromosome joins with the egg, then a baby boy will develop.

Identical twins share the same genes.

'It's in your genes'

Genes determine what a baby looks like. Genes also determine whether a baby will inherit certain diseases. Conditions such as **cystic fibrosis** and **haemophilia** are passed on through families.

How are twins made?

There are two kinds of twins. Fraternal twins are made when two separate eggs are fertilized at the same time. These twins don't look the same. They can be different sexes. Identical twins are made when an egg splits into two after fertilization. These twins are the same sex and look identical.

Early Development

The egg and sperm join and form one cell. A few hours later the cell splits in half. Then these new cells split to create four cells. The cells keep splitting until a ball of cells is formed. This ball of cells is called the blastocyst.

This diagram shows the journey of the fertilized egg. It turns into a ball of cells called a blastocyst.

The journey of the blastocyst

The blastocyst forms more cells. As it does this, it travels down the **fallopian tube**. It takes about seven days to reach the uterus. By now it is made up of about a hundred cells. The blastocyst burrows into the soft lining of the uterus. The centre of the blastocyst contains cells that will grow into a baby.

The placenta

The cells on the outside of the blastocyst join the wall of the uterus. They form an organ called the **placenta**. The placenta provides the baby with food and oxygen from its mother.

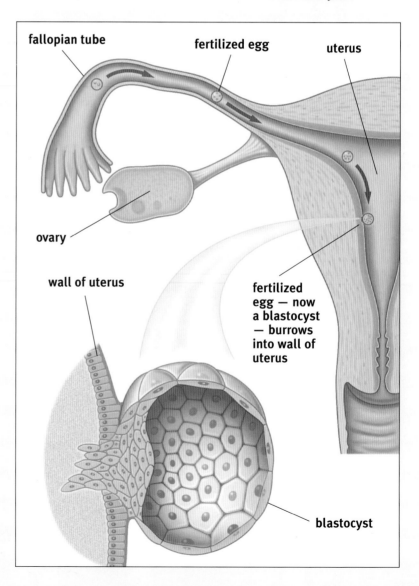

fallopian tube

fertilized egg

uterus

ovary

wall of uterus

fertilized egg — now a blastocyst — burrows into wall of uterus

blastocyst

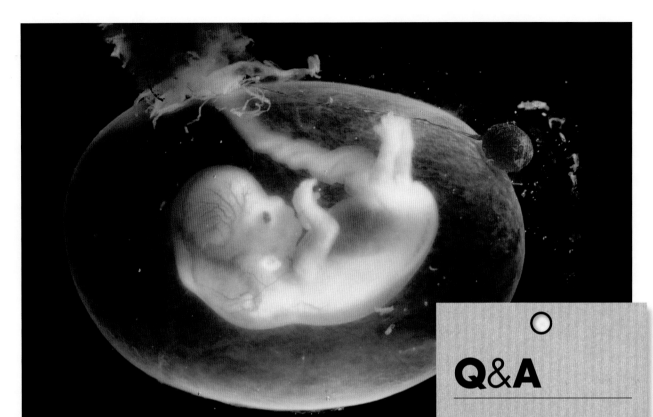

This embryo is about seven or eight weeks old. It already has eyes and limbs.

The new baby
Doctors have different names for the growing baby. For the first eight weeks of its life inside its mother they call it an embryo. After eight weeks and until it is born, they call it a **foetus**.

Changes to the mother
Many changes happen to a woman's body when she is having a baby. Her periods usually stop. Her breasts may grow bigger and feel uncomfortable. This is because they are preparing to make milk. At first, many women feel tired and nauseous (sick).

Q&A

What is a miscarriage?
In the early stages of pregnancy, some women have what seems like a very heavy and painful period. This is the body getting rid of the baby and the lining of the uterus. It is called a miscarriage. Miscarriages may happen because the embryo or foetus dies. Many women who have a miscarriage have a healthy baby next time they get pregnant.

The **Developing Baby**

At eight weeks the **foetus** already looks a little like a baby. It measures about 2.5 centimetres long and weighs two grams. The heart and lungs are formed. It can even move its arms and legs. By 12 weeks the foetus is about 7.5 centimetres long and weighs about 18 grams. Its head is much bigger than its body. The ears and eyelids are already formed.

Taking care

The growing baby floats inside a sac filled with fluid. This protects the baby from the outside world. Many things can affect the way the baby develops. To help the baby grow properly, the mother should eat well. She should also avoid smoking, taking drugs and drinking alcohol.

placenta

cervical canal

cervix

anus

vagina

umbilical cord

uterus

urethra

A woman and foetus in the final week of pregnancy.

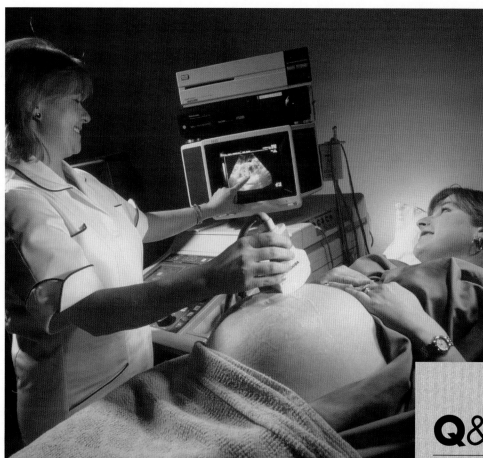

Some people find out if they are having a girl or a boy at an ultrasound scan.

Sixteen to twenty weeks

The baby grows quickly between 16 and 20 weeks. By 20 weeks the mother is rounder and looks pregnant. The baby is about 25 centimetres long. It is kicking and doing somersaults. Many mothers feel the baby move for the first time.

Ready for the birth

Most babies are ready to be born at around 40 weeks. Many of them will have turned upside down. Their heads point down towards the cervix (the opening at the bottom of the uterus). Some babies are born premature. This means they are born before 37 weeks. Premature babies need special care at a hospital.

Q&A

What is an ultrasound?

Doctors use ultrasound scans to see the unborn baby. Scans use high-frequency sound waves. These bounce off the baby and make a picture. Doctors can take measurements of the baby from this picture. They can find out if the baby is developing properly.

Giving Birth

The baby is usually born when the pregnant woman's body Is ready. The uterus begins to tighten and squeeze its muscles. This squeezing action pushes the baby out of the mother's body. These squeezes and pushes are called contractions. The time from when the contractions start to when the baby is born is called labour.

Hard work

Labour is another name for work. During labour the contractions get stronger and closer together. They can also become more painful. A **midwife** encourages the mother to push. She also checks that mother and baby are well during the birth.

The baby's journey

The contractions push the baby's head from the uterus into the cervix. The cervix opens up. It opens wider to let the baby's head enter the mother's vagina. The vagina then stretches to let the baby out of its mother. Sometimes **forceps** or a **ventouse extractor** is used to pull the baby out.

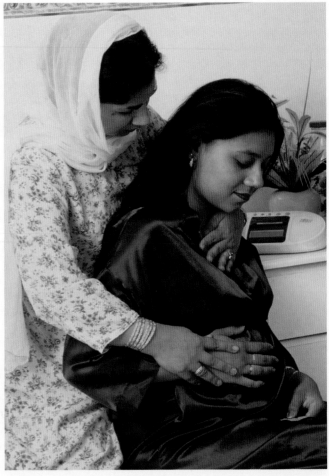

Labour can last a couple of hours or a few days.

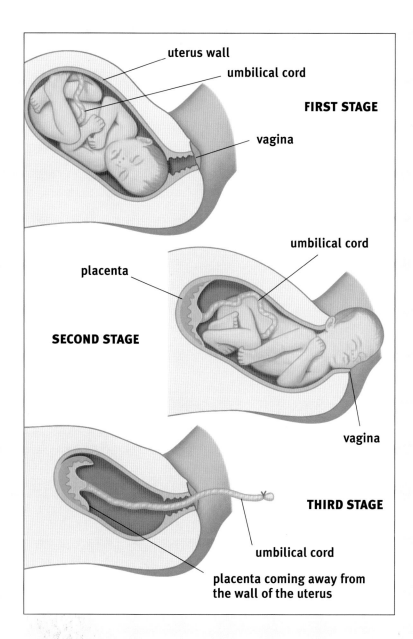

uterus wall

umbilical cord

FIRST STAGE

vagina

umbilical cord

placenta

SECOND STAGE

vagina

THIRD STAGE

umbilical cord

placenta coming away from
the wall of the uterus

The three
stages of
labour.

First breaths

When the baby is born, it takes its first breath.
Many babies start to cry. These cries help make the
baby breathe and take oxygen from the air. Until
now the baby has taken oxygen from the **placenta**
and **umbilical cord**. The doctor or midwife clamps
and cuts the umbilical cord. This separates the baby
from the placenta. Finally, the mother pushes out
the placenta and umbilical cord.

Q&A

What is a caesarean?

Sometimes babies are
born by an operation
called a caesarian. When
this happens, the mother
is given an **anaesthetic**.
The surgeon makes a cut
through the mother's
stomach into the uterus.
The baby and placenta are
gently taken out. Doctors
decide to do a caesarean
when they are worried
about the health of the
mother or baby.

A Baby's **First Year**

Most newborn babies are about 50 centimetres long. They weigh between three and three and a half kilograms. They can see and hear. When they feel hungry, thirsty or uncomfortable, they will cry.

Feeding

Newborn babies' digestive systems cannot deal with solid food yet. Mothers produce milk in their breasts for the babies to drink. The newborn baby suckles at her breast automatically. In the first days after the birth the mother produces a liquid called colostrum. It is very thick and full of **nutrients**. After a few days, breast milk appears. This contains everything the baby needs to be healthy.

Formula milk

Not all mothers are able to breastfeed their babies. Some mothers choose to give formula milk. This is made from cows' milk. It is fed to the baby by a bottle. After six months, most babies can begin to eat some solid foods.

A baby can suckle from its mother's breast as soon as it's born.

This baby is six months old. He can stand up with help from his father.

○

Q&A

How do babies learn to talk?

Some scientists think babies learn to talk by copying people around them. Other scientists think that babies learn to talk automatically. Most toddlers can say a few simple words when they are aged between 12 and 18 months.

Growing babies

By three months most babies can hold up their heads. They make noises when they are talked to, and grab toys. At six months most babies can sit up with help. They can pick up toys and put things in their mouth.

Most nine-month-old babies can crawl. Many can stand if they hold onto something. They can also hold a cup. By 12 months some babies start to walk and say a few words.

Growing Up

Children grow quickly in the first 18 months of life. This is their first growth spurt. Between 18 months and five years old their growth slows down. They learn physical skills such as running and kicking a ball. Gradually, children get more control over their bodies. From five onwards they get better at activities such as swimming, ball sports and dancing.

Puberty

Puberty is the time when children's bodies start to become more like adult bodies. Their reproductive **organs** start growing. They also have a second growth spurt. Puberty in girls often starts between 11 and 13. Puberty in boys usually happens a few years after girls. At this time young people find their moods and feelings change a lot. The changes to their bodies may make them feel awkward and clumsy.

These pictures show young people before and after puberty.

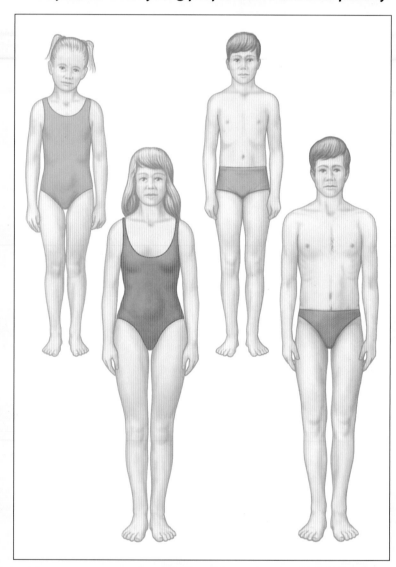

Girls

When girls reach puberty, their breasts begin to grow and their hips look more rounded. They grow pubic hair and hair under their arms. Their periods usually start around this time too. Their reproductive organs are getting ready to work.

Doctors can help to make teenage acne better with special creams and medicine.

Boys

When boys reach puberty, their muscles usually get bigger. Their voices get deeper. They grow pubic hair and hair under their arms. They also grow hair on their faces, legs, arms and chests. Their reproductive organs begin to produce sperm.

Q&A

Why do teenagers get acne?

During puberty, girls and boys have extra **hormones** in their blood. These hormones can create more oil, called **sebum**. This oil can block the pores on the face. This means **bacteria** can get trapped in the pores. When this happens, the bacteria can grow and cause spots, or acne.

Relationships and **Feelings**

The first relationships babies and children are likely to have are with their parents and family. Most children share strong feelings of love with their family. As they get older they meet people outside the family. They form relationships with friends, teachers or other people they meet. They will experience many different feelings for these people.

It is natural for young people to have sexual feelings for one another.

Keeping healthy relationships

Relationships that make us feel happy, respected and confident can be called successful or healthy relationships. Sometimes people get into relationships that make them feel confused and unhappy. Perhaps they are forced to do things that are wrong. These relationships are unhealthy. Anyone involved in this kind of relationship should ask someone they trust for help.

Sexual attraction

During puberty it is natural to feel sexually attracted to other young people. **Hormones** are released into the body that make people want to get close to other boys or girls. They may want to hug and kiss them. These feelings are natural and part of being human.

In a healthy relationship no one should feel forced to do anything they don't want to.

Sexual relationships

Sometimes young people feel pressured to have sexual intercourse. Nobody should start a sexual relationship until they are ready. A good sexual relationship is built on trust, respect and care for the other person's feelings.

Q&A

What is a homosexual relationship?

A relationship between a male and female is called a heterosexual relationship. Sometimes two men or two women are sexually attracted to each other. This is called a homosexual relationship. These can also be called gay or lesbian relationships.

Birth Control

Birth control is also known as contraception. If people want to avoid having a baby, there are many different methods of contraception from which to choose.

Condoms

Condoms are made out of thin rubber. They fit over an erect penis. Condoms should be put on before the penis goes inside the vagina. They catch sperm when the man ejaculates. Condoms are available from pharmacies and supermarkets. They are also available free at family planning clinics.

Birth control pills

Doctors can prescribe birth control pills. These pills have **hormones** that stop the ovaries from releasing eggs. There are also emergency birth control pills. These should be taken if somebody has had sex without using contraception. The pills must be taken within 72 hours of having sex.

Birth control pills are a very effective form of contraception. They must be taken exactly as the doctor prescribes.

Doctors and family planning clinics give advice about birth control to young people.

Intrauterine device

A doctor can fit an intrauterine device (**IUD**) inside a woman's uterus. The IUD stops sperm and eggs from joining together.

Diaphragm

Women can use a small plastic cap called a **diaphragm**. It fits over the cervix to stop the sperm from getting in. Diaphragms are available in different sizes. Doctors must make sure the diaphragm fits properly.

Natural forms of contraception

The withdrawal method is when a man takes his penis out of the vagina before he ejaculates. The rhythm method is when a couple don't have sex around the days when the egg is ready to be fertilized. Both of these methods can be unreliable.

Q&A

What is abstinence?

Abstinence means not having sex, even if you really want it. Many young people are in love but decide not to have sex. They decide to wait until they are married. They believe this is the best way to avoid getting pregnant.

Sexually Transmitted Infections

Diseases spread by sexual intercourse or by touching people sexually are called sexually transmitted infections (STIs). An example of an STI is pubic lice, or crabs. These parasites are usually passed through close body contact. There are many other more serious STIs.

Bacterial STIs

Syphilis, **gonorrhoea** and **chlamydia** are STIs caused by **bacteria**. Patients can be treated with medicines called antibiotics. If these illnesses are left untreated, people can become very ill. Women can become infertile.

Herpes and warts

Herpes is an STI caused by a virus. Infected people get sores on and around the sex **organs**. There is no cure. Medicines make the sores go away for a while. Another virus causes **genital warts**. The warts can be treated but they often return.

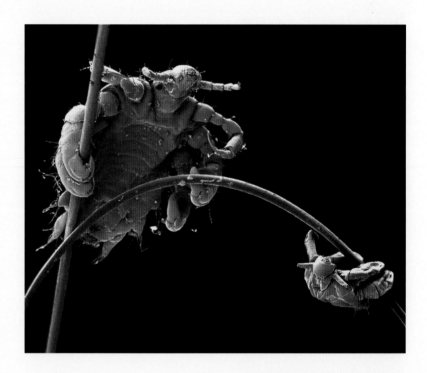

Pubic lice can be caused by sexual contact and poor hygiene.

Hepatitis B

Hepatitis B is caused by a virus. It affects the liver and can make someone very ill. It is passed through infected blood. There is no cure for hepatitis B but there is a **vaccine** that helps to prevent the disease.

There is no cure for AIDs. Throughout the world people are campaigning to try and find one.

HIV/AIDS

HIV (Human Immunodeficiency Virus) is a serious STI. HIV can live in semen or fluid from the vagina. It can be spread by infected blood. It is not spread by coughing, hugging or greeting somebody with a kiss.

The HIV virus can live in someone's body for years before they become ill. Eventually it turns into **AIDS** (Acquired Immune Deficiency Syndrome). A person with AIDS cannot fight infection and eventually dies.

Q&A

What is safer sex?

Safer sex is also called protected sex. People can protect themselves from STIs by using a condom. Safer sex is also about being honest. People should always let their sexual partners know if they have an STI.

Glossary

AIDS — Short for 'Acquired Immune Deficiency Syndrome'. People eventually get AIDS if they have been infected with the HIV virus. People die from AIDS because their bodies cannot fight infection.

amoebae — Tiny, single-celled animals that live in water and soil. Most amoebae can be seen only with a microscope.

anaesthetic — A drug that is given to someone before an operation to stop them from feeling pain.

bacteria — Single-celled organisms that can cause disease. Good bacteria help keep people healthy.

blood vessels — Narrow tubes in the body through which the blood flows.

chlamydia — A sexually transmitted infection that is caused by bacteria. Untreated chlamydia can cause infertility.

chromosomes — Strands of information contained in the sex cells.

cystic fibrosis — An inherited disease that makes the body create too much mucus.

diaphragm — A method of birth control. A small plastic cap is fitted over the cervix to prevent sperm from finding an egg to fertilize.

DNA — Short for 'deoxyribonucleic acid'. A chemical that makes up the chromosomes and holds genetic information.

fallopian tubes — The tubes down which the eggs travel to be fertilized.

foetus — The medical name for a baby that has been in the uterus for longer than eight weeks.

forceps — A surgical instrument that looks like a pair of tongs. It is used for pulling or lifting the baby out of the woman's body.

genes — Packages of information attached to the chromosomes that decide what a baby will be like.

genital warts — A sexually transmitted infection that causes warts to form on the genitals (the external reproductive organs). There is no cure.

gonorrhoea — A sexually transmitted infection caused by bacteria. It can cause infertility.

haemophilia — An inherited disease that stops blood from clotting properly.

HIV — Short for 'Human Immunodeficiency Virus'. An incurable STI that eventually turns into AIDS.

hormones — Chemicals in the body that trigger events such as birth, puberty and menstruation.

IUD — Short for 'intrauterine device'. A method of birth control in which a doctor inserts a small device into the uterus. The IUD is designed to prevent a sperm and egg from joining together.

Further Information

midwife	A nurse who is specially trained to help when a baby is being born.
nutrients	The parts of your food, such as vitamins and minerals, that are important for growth and development.
organs	Parts of the body that do a particular job.
placenta	The organ connected to the wall of the uterus during pregnancy. It provides the baby with oxygen and nourishment.
sebum	An oil produced by the glands in the skin. During puberty, too much sebum may be produced. This clogs the pores and causes acne.
syphilis	A very infectious and dangerous STI. If left untreated, it can kill the infected person.
umbilical cord	A cord that travels from the placenta to the baby's abdomen. It carries food and oxygen to the baby.
vaccine	A medicine that is injected or given by mouth to protect someone from disease.
ventouse extractor	A vacuum device or suction cup that is used to help deliver a baby.

Books

Body Science: The Human Lifecycle
by Rufus Bellamy (Franklin Watts, 2004)
How Does My Body Work: What Happens When We Are Born and Grow
by Jacqui Bailey (Wayland, 2007)
Kingfisher Knowledge: Human Body
by Richard Walker (Kingfisher, 2006)
Our Bodies: Reproduction
by Steve Parker (Wayland, 2004)
The Oxford Children's A to Z of the Human Body
by Bridget and Neil Ardley (Oxford University Press, 2003)
Usborne Internet-Linked Complete Book of the Human Body by Anna Claybourne (Usborne Publishing, 2003)

Websites

www.innerbody.com (click on pictures of male and female reproductive systems)
kidshealth.org/kid/grow/body_stuff/puberty.html
kidshealth.org/kid/health_problems/infection/hiv.html
www.bbc.co.uk/science/humanbody/body/index.shtml
(click on links under the heading 'Puberty')

Index

Page numbers in **bold** refer to illustrations.